POEMS FROM INDIRA

REFLECTIONS
through Life's
Hourglass

POEMS FROM INDIRA

REFLECTIONS
through Life's Hourglass

CLIFF RATZA

Poems from Indira
Reflections through Life's Hourglass
Copyright © 2020 by **Cliff Ratza**. All rights reserved.

Library of Congress Control Number: 2020922803
ISBN: Paperback: 978-1-7361828-0-2

No part of this publication may be reproduced, stored in a retrieval system or transmitted in any way by any means, electronic, mechanical, photocopy, recording or otherwise without the prior permission of the author except as provided by USA copyright law.

This is a work of fiction. Names, characters, businesses, places, events and incidents are either the products of the author's imagination or used in a fictitious manner. Any resemblance to actual persons, living or dead, or actual events is purely coincidental.

The opinions expressed by the author are not necessarily those of Lightning Brain Press.

Published in the United States of America.

Published by Lightning Brain Press
1. Fantasy (General)
2. Science

Contents

About the Poems: 1
About the Writer: 3
The Simple Scholar 4
Beyond a Shadow 5
Wisdom's Wondrous Font 6
Against the Current...7
More or Less 8
The Wisdom of Youth 9
Trilogy 11
Into the Void...11
The Quiet Realm 13
Return of the King 14
For Sister-One-and-Only..16
Captain Bill 17
Octavio's Gift..18
Simple Pleasures...19
Confessions of a Fitness Addict 20
Another Season 21
Returning to Life...22
The Spiral Stairway...23
Song without Words 25
The Doubter's Prison...26
Ebenezer's Epiphany 27
The Dawn Patrol 28
Serendipity's Kiss 29
September Song 30

Autumn Splendor	31
Cleanup Man!	32
Simply Irresistible	33
Last Man Standing	34
The Winter Coat	35
The Children's Hour	36
The Nerve of Youth	37
The Pretender	38
In the Groove	39
The Illusion	40
Turn the Page	41
Passages	42
On the Beach	43
View from the Top	44
The Key of Life	45
The Once and Future	46
Free to Choose	47
To the Point	48
The Care-Filled Traveler	49
The Magic Path	50
The Epiphany	51
I Run to You	52
Searching for a Lesser God	53
Summer Solstice	55
Winter Solstice	57
Letting Go	58
Break Out	59
The Second Coming	60
Whither Sunrise	61
Brave News World	62
Shadows of Joy	63
Seize the Day	64

Mere Humanity	65
Being in America	66
Whither the Gods	68
Autumn Perfection	69
Vital Lies	70
Next in Line	71
The Abyss	72
The Mystical Memory Garden	73
A Special Place	74
Home Field Advantage	75
Truth be Told	76
Apprehensions from A Nether Place	77
After the Fall	78
The Transcendental Man	79
The Lost Word	80
Vanishing Point	81
The Siren's Song	82
The Road Less Traveled	83
Mediocrity's Stepchild	84
Great Expectations	85
Just Do It	86
Past Remembrance	87
Shelter from the Storm	88
Make the Most	89
Time to Go	90

About the Poems:

Readers of "The Lightning Brain Series" know that Electra Kittner and Indira Ramanujan are Kindred Spirits in heart and soul, just as I am Indira's Kindred Spirit in poetry. She is the "Inner Voice" for the poems in my novels, and I hope you enjoy them.

Poetry and literature require a depth of maturity gained only by experiencing life's events and emotions firsthand. Unlike either Electra or Indira, I skated on the surface in my earlier years, avoiding those dangerous spots where we can fall through and drown. But the flip side is that if we survive, we surface with a deeper understanding of life.

I have reached a point where I am better able to reflect on the World about us from a first-person perspective. I enjoy turning my observations into verse. They cover many areas, all part of that emergent experience called living. Some are light and whimsical, others more serious. They're written in a modern lyrical or metaphysical style using meter and rhyming schemes that communicate in a clear and engaging manner.

About the Writer:

Cliff Ratza would describe himself as a "simple scholar" who enjoys putting into verse his views on "the Human Condition." His poems are written on the run while thoughts occur as he moves through the day. He teaches at Chicago area universities, which he combines with business and writing careers. He hopes you find at least some of his poems enjoyable or useful, and he will be pleased if you do.

The Simple Scholar

I'd say that I'm mediocre,
In all I've aspired to be.
And though I have tried it can't be denied,
What's lacking is profundity.

But still I can study life's drama,
And consider from singular view.
Wise persons may find they've left nothing behind,
My wish simple wisdom shows through.

Beyond a Shadow

(for Groundhogs everywhere)

Whether or not there's a shadow,
Better weather and days are in store.
And if they take longer to get here,
You'll appreciate them even more.

Wisdom's Wondrous Font

Minds hold many a syllable,
They float like a dirigible.
Sometimes they bump and form a clump,
Results are unpredictable.

But sometimes they will form,
Advice beyond the norm.
When that's the case do not erase,
Some wisdom has been born.

So when you find that's true,
Here's what you must do.
Tuck it away for another day,
Awaiting to help you.

Against the Current

Fight long as you can the tug of time's tide,
Irresistible force we're unable to hide.
It gives you a feeling of Life unfilled,
While taking away what you wanted to build.

Whither the struggle to where will it lead?
Penultimate victory is not ours indeed.
And if senses are tricked to reliving the past,
It's a cruel illusion that simply won't last.

But resist for the challenge do not look behind,
Life's journey insisting you must use your mind.
Though winding to where we eventually fall,
By then not to worry your spirit's seen all.

More or Less

I only am one more or less,
To me it's about the same.
Try my best like all the rest,
And enjoy being part of the game.

But nimble Youth has ego aglow,
It matters what others think.
The World must know they're best in show,
So they push right to the brink.

The World applauds then turns away,
Leaving lessons for Youth to learn.
The World changes unpredictably,
Now a different player's turn.

The Wisdom of Youth

Youth's intoxicating optimism will not be denied!
Unstoppable force, it powers that wild ride,
One-way, once-in-a-lifetime trip to boundless future.
Just over time's horizon, the other side
Of breathless dreams, nothing can circumscribe!

So they leap with brazen certainty,
Targeting their destiny,
But where do they arrive?
Too oft it's not what dreams foretold,
Doubts start to grow as blood runs cold,
They struggle to survive.

Or so the Elders say.
Heed our words you must delay,
Your journey to another day.
Youth says No please let us go!
Here's what we must do,
Hurry and scurry to reach for the stars,
Or miss our rendezvous.

Wise Athena who is right?
Or is there middle ground.
What words of wisdom will calm both sides,
And turn their heads around.

She turns first to the Elders,
With wry smile starts to say.
Think back to when you were their age,
Behold that you are they!

Next to Youth her charm she turns,
Your dream might not come true.
If that's what you find have another in mind,
Something that's calling to you.

And so we've come full circle,
Youth's wisdom now shows through.
Young and Old are both as one,
Their journey makes it true.

Trilogy

(Three Poems regarding Remorse, Remembrance and Renewal)

Into the Void

A dreaded darkness fills me to the core,
I grope for bearings to help pull free.
My pole star lost - I have been tossed
and alone now must cross,
This leaden, deadened, mirthless sea.

The harboring lights of my once
carefree youth are gone,
Through no one's fault save that of unrelenting Time.
And though often told that this loss would unfold,
No preparation could soften or
lessen or put in remission,
This grief I am feeling that sends my soul reeling,
This loss of the precious that cuts to the bone,
This loss of the priceless that's all mine to own.

But stop to remember light comes back in view,
When Love of the child burns bright and cuts through
The fog of gloom.
My Spirit restored to be happy again?
I numb and dumb wait for the if and the when.

The Quiet Realm

A peaceful stillness fills the room,
That bustled once with life.
Like King and Queen their children seen,
My peerless Man and Wife.

This Kingdom of those no longer near,
For those who care to see.
No more adorned by mortal form,
Their Spirits are set free.

Though Time demanded they depart,
For fields far from here.
Their presence will forever thrill,
A mind's eye holds them near.

And those of you yet to pass through,
That somber loss above,
Perhaps assured grief partly cured,
By grace of lasting love.

Return of the King

The King and his Fair Lady,
I sense return to me.
This grace-filled gift my Spirits lift,
Awaken now and see.

I have weathered the worst winter,
That obscured the path once known.
Though departure caused by Nature's laws,
It struck with a fury sufficient to bury,
This untested person uncertain and wary,
It left me all alone.

But now comes Spring heralding the King,
The returning royal pair.
My senses shout they are about,
The signs are everywhere.

I see them in the duet
Of swiftly soaring swooping songbirds,
This aerial ballet.
The nest they build with family filled,
Which offspring can't repay.

I feel them in the emergent emerald stems
Of dew-jeweled garden flowers,
Now bursting forth I find.

Roots nurtured firmly in the soil,
Their essence intertwined.

I hear them in the gentle burbling
Of fresh fragrant breezes,
Rustling softly through the trees.
They teach they guide they have not died!
They're not yet done with me.

But will King and Lady-In-Waiting-No-More,
Dwell evermore in me?
Or will they fade like late Autumn shade,
The ghosts of memory?

The answer lies unknown for now,
Locked in a vault of mind.
To which I say on rare Spring day,
Winter stay far behind!

For Sister-One-and-Only

There is no doubt about me for you,
Saucy Sister oh so fair.
No matter what fortune deals our way,
You'll find I'm always there.

Though we are very different,
Apparent from either side,
The love that binds remains through time,
It's buried deep inside.

Do not fret be too upset,
When we dicker or disagree.
We'll have our say won't walk away,
Tomorrow Gods referee.

Emotions are strictly a private affair,
So reluctant to put on display.
But if ever you doubt please hear verses out,
My feelings assuredly stay.

Captain Bill

Captain Bill's my singular friend.
When describing him I find,
It takes two literary characters,
Their nature intertwined.

The first is the seafaring captain,
Jack Aubrey is his name.
The second jolly old Fezziwig,
Whom Dickens brought to fame.

Aubrey shows what friendship means,
And how to handle stress.
Fezziwig shows that even work woes,
Won't stand in the way of success.

If ever you meet Captain William,
A suggestion for what you might offer.
A cheerful toast you might propose,
Let's all live long and prosper!

Octavio's Gift

They can't be bought they can't be sold,
They stretch beyond the years.
They grow in strength as you grow old,
Friendship through laughter and tears.

It's hard to explain its genesis,
A gift right from the start.
Resulting perhaps from synthesis,
Akin to till death do us part.

How many will Fate send on your way?
Small number that's unknown.
Stay alert invite them in,
Or else end up alone.

Simple Pleasures

(For Kathi)

Warm sunlight streaming
From your radiant smiling face.
The murmur of family voices
At familiar time or place.

Home-cooked supper fragrance
After rushing through the day.
Such are simple pleasures
Hands of time won't take away.

Life sends these mini-gifts to us
Too oft too busy to see.
It takes a turning point or two
For better clarity.

Pleasant morsels all about
They are for us to taste.
They wish to please they seek us out
Don't let them go to waste.

Confessions of a Fitness Addict

I'm a persnickety sniping fitness snob,
Pleading guilty to the charge.
I snicker at fitness wannabes,
Whose bodies are much too large.

To wide-body women with runway ambition,
You provide a revealing sight.
I silently gape at the rearranged shape,
When you pack into jeans much too tight.

And to guys who have paunches
overflowing their haunches,
There's a lot that I could say to you.
When standing behind a thought comes to mind,
Move over you're blocking the view.

And what about me this cantankerous fool,
Whose views are so silly and tart?
Don't pay me much mind look closely you'll find,
I'm worn out and falling apart!

Another Season

Another season waits for you,
But when there's no control.
It whirls you to some stranger place,
No help or supporting role.

Onset has causes disaster and losses,
Emotions are under attack.
As you awaken and stare at surreal nightmare,
You realize there's no going back.

But there's hope for recovery for you will survive,
Wherever however you land.
The life that you make and the path that you take,
Are held in your still-trembling hand.

Shaken but wiser beginning to see,
The illusion that you're in control.
No matter how careful risk will imperil,
Remember whatever your goal.

Returning to Life

As you travel through Life you're likely to find,
Rare items that you'd like to own.
Regarding this Fate's quite unkind,
They only are on loan.

Fame and Fortune give you a wink,
You're picked for the grand prize.
But no matter how clever you think or do,
Can't keep it from shrinking in size.

And what about the most precious possession,
Your family and friends seen each day.
The Gods are stone-faced there is no concession,
To prevent being taken away.

Danger to think you can keep what you earned,
Life says all must be returned.

The Spiral Stairway

We each explode into the world,
On a trajectory all our own.
Ignited by our parent's love,
A gift for us alone.

Intending you to reach your dream,
With the promises it holds.
That golden bold ascent begins,
Star-bound odyssey unfolds.

Onward upward so you go,
Stepping higher and higher.
Surpassing all the boundaries,
An ever-widening gyre.

But then one day an odd event,
You're suddenly startled to find,
The arc's no longer upward bound,
The apex is behind.

But don't despair the downward stair,
There's an opportunity.
To better view what you've come through,
And assess reality.

The mind's eye sees more clearly now,
It's the lens you see life through.
How sharp becomes the focal point,
That answer's left for you.

Dwell only briefly in the past,
Don't rest on laurels won.
Better to inhabit now,
And build on what's been done.

And if you give back more to those,
No matter who they be.
A priceless gift awaits for you,
Glimpse immortality.

Song without Words

They come like tree-leaf shadows
On bright windy Summer day.
Butterfly-like dancing
On half-curtained window bay.
Penetrating senses like a mesmerizing charm.
A streaming wordless melody
That will silence false alarm.

Some forgotten sight or sound
That resonates in our mind.
And spirits us away to some place left far behind.
Like intuition - premonition impossible to trace.
It causes shiver - senses quiver
With neither name nor face.

We're suspended but a moment
That's transfixed in unknown space,
The spell dissolves abruptly
We are freed but sense its grace.
The feeling quickly floats away
Leaving but a gentle sigh.
The kind we hear when wisps of mist
Curl insouciantly toward the sky.

The Doubter's Prison

For those who have conviction and faith,
Their journey sure their sleep secure.
Compared to me doubt comes as wraith,
Haunting this life I must endure.

I curse the loss of innocence,
Replaced with jaded adult views.
Skepticism - indifference,
The path becomes so hard to choose.

But while I'm trapped by my own doubt,
I will not quit I carry on.
I'll strive for more convincing thought,
Perhaps I will break free anon.

Ebenezer's Epiphany

Cry-out for those you pushed away!
Cry-out for gifts you refused to pay!
Cry-out for chances thrown away!
Cry-out for what you did not say!

Too late too late to make amends,
Time expires your story ends.
This is how the faint heart rends,
A just reward the harsh truth sends.

Cry-out to no one but to me,
Insignificant speck on a sullen sea.
Futile tears flow silently,
Invisible as you now will be.

But stop this deathly cold nightmare!
Awaken now and make repair.
Mend the errors if you dare,
Reverse the cry-outs show you care.

The Dawn Patrol

(A Labor Day Salute)

Swish Swish – it's the Farmer Who is up and now about.
Clank Clank – sounds the factory
worker turning products out.
Crush Crush – it's the commuter on
his trek to work each day.
Rush Rush – goes the driver passing him along the way.

Welcome to the Dawn Patrol they're up before the Sun.
Like pieces of a puzzle they fit to get work done.
They number in the millions if you
knew each one you'd see.
They're experts in the roles they play
and share common destiny.

Their collective will's unstoppable they have an energy.
That says all things are possible as a people always free.
So when the day is over and daily bread's been won.
I give thanks to solidarity and happy to be among.

Serendipity's Kiss

Oh for those moments that take our breath away
And leave us suspended in the timeless
presence of their being!
Search your memory, find them if you can,
And you will see their magic, turning
eternity into but a single day.

But do not live for just these alone.
Serendipity blows you a kiss and they float your way,
Crossing your path on an ordinary day
for you to seize the moment.
How many? How often? To the Gods only known.

Alas, they silently come wrapped in disguise.
Revealed only when peeked inside to find
A gift that surprises, mesmerizes, we must act now!
No second chance given to recapture the prize.

But what about those ordinary moments of our days?
Don't discard them, they are magic
too - just a slower-acting kind.
It likely takes more living for their import to emerge,
For then you'll say quotidian days have power to amaze.

September Song

I shall always remember the Song of September,
 As calendar months parade by.
Heard in the soft soothing voice of my Father,
 And with it my brief poignant sigh.

Written by dervishes whirling away,
 We're like wind-blown leaves in a storm.
Though the fury has past their impact will last,
 Though now in a gentler form.

A cascading connection of watershed marks,
 That sketch what I look like today.
Some happy some sad most make my heart glad,
 Time's flow will not sweep them away.

And though your September is different from mine,
 Its tune resonates just as true.
So listen for theme song that whispers your name,
 As it once again echoes anew.

Autumn Splendor

I sense Autumn's mortality,
Finally able to see.
The dimming light and chilly night,
Portend its destiny.

Joyous Spring and endless Summer,
Both have given way,
And Autumn too will fade from view,
Replaced by Winter gray.

But Autumn days are special gifts,
Awareness has been raised.
Blazing leaves and bright blue skies,
All Nature sings their praise.

And like the Seasons so is Life,
We come and then we go,
Predicting next is but a guess,
Not even the wisest know.

So always remember Autumn splendor,
Hold its meaning tight,
Breathe in deeply don't exhale,
Savor its glorious sight.

Cleanup Man!

Enough's enough there's too much stuff!
Your life has too many things.
Day after day they clutter the way,
It's time to cut the strings.

Possessions ideas and erstwhile friends,
Dragged along all these years.
Time to let go by now you know,
No one will shed any tears.

Once they were important to you,
But now your life has changed.
So don't delay - discard today,
It's time to rearrange.

Don't know what to keep or throw?
Just start pitching - look out below!

Simply Irresistible

KO absolute anon.
Exit from the lexicon.
Strike it out we're moving on.
Simply Irreversible!

Absolute a zero score.
Relative moves to the fore.
Pundits use it more and more.
Simply so implausible!

Now that absolute is gone.
Compromise no longer wrong.
All in D.C. get along?
Simply unbelievable!

D.C. a mess - the country ill,
We the People had our fill.
Clean out Houses on the Hill?
Simply irresistible!

Last Man Standing

Last man standing,
That's what you want to be.
You've grabbed the ring and all it brings,
You've clinched the victory.
Praise and cheer they fill the air,
Your name is spoken everywhere,
The world is at your feet.

But in the contest of your Life,
Standing last cuts like a knife,
Who'll be there to care?
There's emptiness since friends are gone,
There's struggle finding where you belong,
There's no clear path in sight.

So if your standing wish comes true,
Better prepare for what to do,
For how to carry on.
My advice at least for now,
Live in the present here is how.
Blend the best of old and new,
That's the best I can offer you.

The Winter Coat

A visitor arrives each year,
Wrapped in a coat of gray.
No invite needed warning heeded,
His cloak proclaims his stay.

It covers up now barren land,
Like a blanket that's off-white.
And reaching upward towards the sky,
Overcast blocks Sun from sight.

If you do not prepare for him,
His cover may smother you.
Don't be depressed just take some steps,
So brightness can shine through.

Search among the gifts he brings,
Pretend some appeal to you.
Try your best convince yourself,
Believe that this is true.

But if you can't repeat this charm,
Sooner or later it shall be warm...

The Children's Hour

Children teach your parents well,
They forgot what kid's can tell.
Youthful faith trumps oldster power,
Show them in your children's hour.

Laser focus at school or play,
Innocence keeps fear away.
Tiny egos don't interfere,
Honesty keeps conscience clear.

The adult world is not as nice,
It needs a dose of childish advice.
Though sometimes hard it's understood,
Grownups learn the things they should.

The Nerve of Youth

Fresh nerve of steel's a treasured gift,
Bestowed in early years.
It makes them swift and makes them sure,
Protects them from their fears.

Alas it does not last too long,
Time wears it away.
When nervous energy runs down,
And caution rules the day.

So propose a toast that Youth runs free,
Have their sights set high.
Give them strength then let them be,
May their power never die.

The Pretender

I wake up each day disappointed to see,
A glance at the mirror's reflection of me.
There must be some error there has to be more,
In order to handle today what's in store.

I'm busy each day searching hard searching long,
To find everything make me smart make me strong.
And though I have found some they still aren't enough,
To say to the World I have all the right stuff.

And so as I march off to tasks still to do,
Praying no one catches on and sees through.
That I'm able to finish the things that must be,
And so I beseech Lord have mercy on me!

In the Groove

The difference between a rut and a groove,
Is merely a matter of taste.
It simply depends on one's point of view,
So do not pass judgment in haste.

Its good when said you're in the groove,
You've settled into full stride.
Each Dawn breaks bright a breathtaking sight,
Life gives a wonderful ride.

But try to avoid being stuck in a rut,
When everything's stale and old.
Find a way to pull yourself out,
Break free by being bold.

Rut or groove - so where are you?
Pause now and then for in-depth view.

The Illusion

Better to live near the surface,
Rather than diving too deep.
So be entertained and happily busy,
With concerns causing no loss of sleep.

We're told that Life holds great meaning,
For us its grand purpose shines through.
But stop to consider what's often delivered,
Deep meaning is hidden from view.

Don't drown in the substance of being,
Return to the surface for air.
Focus on myriad mundane concerns,
The measure of meaning is there.

Turn the Page

Your story is a work in progress,
Written as you pass through.
And if you do not turn the page,
It will be turned for you.

Major changes mark each chapter,
They come and you will know.
Don't try to block the hand of Fate,
When it taps be ready to go.

And like handwriting on the wall,
Can't change it when it's come.
The plot unfolds as the story's told,
As you keep moving on.

Passages

Our one way only odyssey
The path that we are on.
Made up of many passages,
Emerging when running along.

At first we run fast as we can,
To reach a stage-end prize.
We're thrilled but then we speed away,
As another greets our eyes.

But soon we better realize,
The passage not always fun.
And now the truth reveals itself,
Lento – enjoy the run.

Victory is not laurel-bound,
Instead within the race it's found

On the Beach

Rest assured your future shore,
Wash up on golden sand.
Rich or poor or early or late,
The proverbial promised land.

Previous worries swept away,
You're able to start anew.
Time ticking away at a carefree pace,
Reservations are made for you.

This shining opportunity
Can beat all your requests.
Just move from the beach to sites in store,
There'll be a succession of bests.

View from the Top

I sense I've reached a peak in Life,
Duties done no pain or strife.
For goals remaining no sacrifice,
For time and purpose I don't think twice.

Higher peaks have come and gone,
But this is a resplendent Dawn.
The past is closed so I go beyond,
Excitement awaits as I move on.

And so a wish for all of you,
For all the peaks when you pass through.
Your climb has earned a view from the top,
So enjoy your stay at this passing stop.

The Key of Life

I heard the news report it said,
Pianist Van Cliburn has died.
Warning gong sounding in my head,
Why he's not much older than I!

It seems like only a day ago,
He marched home with first prize.
A tragic loss no music will flow,
Uneasy strange feelings arise.

Counting our years is fun at first,
But soon they add up to a frown.
Coming upon the number worst,
From where we must count down.

But the great Van Cliburn's spirit is free,
Safe and sound in mind.
His music stored with magic key,
Unlock all that you find.

From troubling loss I hope to see,
Odd feelings fade away.
Look forward to a legacy,
Leave one come back to play.

The Once and Future

(Founding Fathers Tribute)

Where have all the Great Men gone?
The heroes in your mind.
We need them now to carry on,
They seem so hard to find.

Concealed perhaps when they appear,
Once human just like us.
Revealed in Wisdom's future year,
Though flesh has turned to dust.

Greatness dwells in each of us,
Awaiting the chosen call.
So do when asked without a fuss,
In time your stature's tall.

Free to Choose

(As the World Turns)

Give us our freedom the patriots shout!
Give us our freedom we can't be without!
Bold words spoken bravely they ring clear and true,
But stop to consider when it's facing you.

You must choose the path to take,
And what's needed along the way.
As you struggle to the distant goal,
Temptation could lead astray.

So ask yourself and answer true,
Will my plans lead to the prize?
You must say yes but do not guess,
Prepare with careful eyes.

So heed these words of wisdom,
When striving to be free.
Only you can see things through,
Choose very carefully.

To the Point

It's taken years to understand,
The focal point of Life.
But now I see its majesty,
No more internal strife.

When young we think that all is ours,
The world revolves round us.
And when our whims aren't fully met,
We make a terrible fuss.

But look beyond your selfish self,
For a selfless path that's right
Reach out to those with heavy needs,
Help make their burden light.

The Care-Filled Traveler

Please take the love I give to you,
Kindred Spirit far from me.
It's the part of life I hadn't found,
Till caring set me free.

The World may wonder what's wrong with him,
From this Muse he will retreat.
Time will show for all to know,
You make my life complete.

So I'll travel to you to be with you,
Across the many-a-mile.
I will ensure love shall endure,
My reward's your eternal smile.

The Magic Path

I've found the path worth searching for,
After all these many years.
It's given me the love I keep,
Beyond pale of joy or fears.

I never felt the words of love,
Till grace inflamed my soul.
Against all odds blessed by the Gods,
It's become my quest my goal.

I shall keep it special keep it safe,
I'll renew it every day.
I shall not rest I'll do my best,
So the treasure of caring will stay.

The Epiphany

My new love has revealed to me,
The secret of eternity.
Don't think me strange don't think me odd,
It has shown to me the face of God.

Last night for all the world to see,
I asked for love to stay with me.
No answer needed I know in my heart,
My wish has been granted I've made a new start.

Feelings have risen past what I've known,
By living beyond I am no more alone.
Emotions embrace me I am free of my doubt,
Let me hold them forever let devotion pour out.

I Run to You

I run through hushed stark darkness
Of cold autumnal night.
Impervious to the realities
Of approaching winter's bite.
For you are the guiding wind at my back
That brilliant shining light.
That will always bring me back to you
My thoughts aloft in flight.

Your feelings reach out across the miles
On golden eagle's wings.
And mine to you for the rendezvous
That only devotion brings.
The joy of knowing we're together
A gift bestowed from kings.
Possessing treasure for our souls
A joy that for us sings.

So my commitment is a pledge to you
That can never be undone.
I run to you until I reach
Our El Dorado's Sun.
Our treasure trove that offers us
All the precious hard-won fun
Of knowing you are safe and warm
In a world that has only just begun.

Searching for a Lesser God

My Kindred Spirit left me alone,
In the blink of a memory ago.
Considered a minor tragedy,
You're expected to survive.
Part of the natural order of things,
Your faith keeps you alive.
But for me it took an eternity,
To lessen the staggering blow.

On regular days a subliminal sense,
A somber void lurking there.
I go about life of the usual sort,
Dark memories don't stand in the way.
Then some odd event strikes to the core,
I push it's relentless to stay.
A brief stabbing panic that no one is left,
Who asks or will actually care.

Some time ago I reached out to the World,
To find a substitute Muse.
I went to work on a fishing net,
It's fibers had all the right properties.
I planned the trip and sailed away,
I cast the net boldly into the seas.
But no luck at all just empty and wet,
Not a single Muse to choose.

The problem is Time turned its back,
On the search for my Kindred one.
The World and I have gone separate ways,
It's a harder fit for me.
Maybe we only get one match,
Comes and goes and no more will be.
So you'll have to settle for a lesser God,
If your search continues on.

Summer Solstice

Ephemeral Summer Solstice.
Spring ends with most daylight.
Our westward gaze absorbs last rays.
The Sun submerged from sight.

Thoughts dwell on past encounters.
When other orbs shone bright.
But like the Sun their day is done.
They've passed to that good night.

Try not to wax nostalgic.
To melancholy do not cling.
It's the same for us as everyone.
No matter pawn or king.

Sadness seeps inside us.
Loved voices no longer sing.
We missed our chance for one last dance.
And peace of mind it brings.

Many things taken for granted.
Many things left unsaid.
It's but a meager substitute.
When eulogies are read.

But on this evening hear them,
It happens if your mind.
Will rendezvous with those now past,
Let calendars rewind.

Winter Solstice

We've reached the Winter Solstice,
Shortest day of the year.
Though longest night the stars shine bright,
Aglow with hope and cheer.

Dwindling days are over,
Brightness emerging instead.
Tomorrow's weather getting better,
Good tidings ring out in my head.

Life too holds many a Solstice,
Turning points march into view.
At steadfast pace then turn about face,
Take heart joy's waiting for you.

Letting Go

Abandoning dreams is hard to do,
They give us hope help us pull through.
And lead us to that better day,
While clearing obstacles in the way.

But dreams like Life they too expire,
Some end up sooner on their funeral pyre.
Though sad let go and light the flame,
So the hope-filled seeker can re-aim.

For every dream that in you dies,
Others from the ashes rise.
Have courage when ready and choose one more,
The future reveals what is in store.

Break Out

Human Nature gives to you,
The tools to survive.
You're safely encased in a hard-shell I,
With instructions for staying alive.

Early on this serves you well,
You adjust to what you see.
But you'll see one day you're in the way,
There's more than merely "Me".

Some Dawn this truth may grace your soul,
Effects can't be undone.
Your feelings will know quo vadis grow,
Break out for what's to come.

The Second Coming

The Second Coming's on its way,
In each of us it's found.
Beyond our one-dimensional self,
Reach out to the world around.

This teaching's found in every Faith,
So touching yet hard to feel.
Blocked by an indifferent-appearing world,
That masks what's truly real.

Help lift the veil clear the way,
So connections can come through.
Offer up what's needed most,
For emergent New World view.

Whither Sunrise

(Easter Tidings)

Daylight tumbles darkly into
Deathlike starless night.
A mindless endless void engulfs
Within inchoate fright.

This is all and nothing else
Forevermore to be.
You thrash about - anguish pours out
In cold stygian sea.

But wait! Look deep within your faith
And find that guiding star.
Eternal light restores your sight
And shows you who you are.

And when Sun rises you decide
What the new day will hold.
Your deeds should fill the deepest needs,
The story's not yet told.

Brave News World

Tsunami washes country away,
Sports idol with feet of clay.
Middle East dictator at an end,
CPR saves man's best friend.

How brave this sampling of the news,
Cacophony of many views.
What's important – who can to say?
Focus on truth – where does it lay?

And who am I to sort things out?
Call me Nemo-with-a-Doubt.
Judge carefully the things you see,
For who knows best what there should be?

Shadows of Joy

Think back if you can to those callow years,
Joy dappled your outlook there weren't many tears.
Dawns breaking in sunlight to endless delight,
With firefly evenings a magical sight.

But too soon it happens as Youth must mature,
Life stretches before us enigmas appear.
Joy becomes muted it's apparent to all,
Heavy load on your shoulders to rise or to fall.

Fortune allows afternoons in the Sun,
But joy visits less often past can't be undone.
Welcome the pleasure but still you may find,
Ineffable feelings cast shadows behind.

Seize the Day

Sometimes it's good to simply sit,
And put your thoughts away.
Let senses peer at what is near,
And feelings come what may.

The World keeps spinning merrily,
Indifferent to you.
You still exist but briefly aren't missed,
Obscured by a larger view.

But you're needed in the role you play,
Your time and effort count.
Whether star or small bit part,
You contribute a goodly amount

Then turn your thinking on again,
Humdrum seems better to you.
The break you took gave fresh outlook,
Seize the day restart anew.

Mere Humanity

We each are merely human,
Disappointing to you and me.
We can't transcend the limits of men,
Or grasp infinity.

You'll never know what's matter,
Or divide the brain from mind.
You'll never see reality,
Or unravel space or time.

And so we're stuck with what we are,
Bewildered unable to see.
The path from here remains unclear,
We're victims of what will be.

But is this curse our greatest strength?
Our separate frailty.
But collectively we go beyond,
Our extended humanity.

Being in America

(July 4th Reverie)

Euphoric possibilities,
Awaiting their discoveries,
Emerging as we strive to be,
Willing to risk it all.

Each new dawn breaks impatiently,
Cloaked with intriguing mystery,
Tempting with uncertainty,
We answer the siren's call.

And so it's been through history,
For nations great and small.
Some served better and gave back more,
Until their fateful fall.

The arrow of Time's in America,
A beacon in the dark.
But will America endure,
Has the archer hit its mark?

America stands proud and tall,
Has weathered every test,
Color- blind clever and practical,
Contingently the best.

Challenge and change are waiting ahead,
With no clear crystal ball,
Outcome's unknown but one thing's been shown,
United - unlikely to fall.

Whither the Gods

Nature's whim demanded more,
Some answers to the World he saw.
His ignorance almost complete,
He conjured up the Gods in awe.

Sometimes they served each other well,
But restless minds would not let be.
Genius probed in Nature's realm,
The Gods unmasked as fantasy.

To help endure indifferent days,
He often clings to vital lies.
Though not as cruel as once before,
The Gods return in different guise.

So until that final setting Sun,
Gods and Man perhaps are one.

Autumn Perfection

The Summer extremes have come and gone,
The promise of Spring has been fulfilled.
The bountiful harvest rolls gently along,
The splendid October as if it were willed.

Autumn perfection it glistens in Sun,
But subliminal sadness sometimes comes to mind.
Are we thankful enough for what has been won?
And what about all that's been left behind?

Spirit sadness to a faraway day,
Enjoy what's been earned as best as you can.
And though burnishing days will wither away,
Look beyond Winter to Spring once again.

Vital Lies

(For the Great Ones)

The World spins round on vital lies,
Fate be damned until one dies.
They power your quest for elusive prize,
Seductively dancing before your eyes.

But you just might have what it takes,
To reach beyond with few mistakes.
If so you become for Humanity,
Persona Immortality.

So keep alive your vital lies,
They give you hope they vitalize.
Your footsteps race past distant years,
Inspiring all - diminishing fears.

Next in Line

You waited for your turn to come,
It did you took that wild ride.
The roller coaster journey's done,
Its time for you to step aside.

Don't be angry no time to grieve,
Think about those next in line.
Their hopes and dreams all they believe,
The time has come for them to shine.

Perhaps there's shelter you can give,
Or sage advice that you can leave.
Nurture Spirits so they live,
Harvest from your Wisdom Tree.

The Abyss

(Look do not leap)

A lurking abyss that you cannot avoid,
Like a moth that is drawn to a flame.
Be careful when peering at puzzling deep,
Hold fast to reality's claim.

Ultimate meaning's a bottomless pit,
A conundrum coiled inside a void.
So ponder but briefly return to the top,
The Gods only briefly annoyed.

Take comfort in knowing that you're not alone,
When probing for what lies below.
For whatever lies shrouded so deep at the bottom,
Forever beyond ours to know.

The Mystical Memory Garden

Tomorrow's memories are made today,
It's good you are too close to see.
Just go about your merry way,
They are a future mystery.

No crystal ball for where things lead,
What fruit your current efforts bring.
Just tend the present plant the seed,
For the flower to bloom and blossoms take wing.

Tomorrow's harvest depends on you,
Its bounty and whether short or long.
So remember today in all that you do,
Blow a kiss to the future keep singing your song.

A Special Place

I hope you have a special place,
Experience there sublime.
Free of three ills of the human race,
Constraints demands and time.

You lost your site when you matured,
In this you had no choice,
But there's another to be heard,
Listen to your inner voice.

You're not allowed to visit long,
Life won't let you stay.
But know the spot you most belong,
It's only a memory away.

Home Field Advantage

It's better to be young than old,
In that we mostly all agree.
Youth can erase mistakes they've made,
And rise to brilliant apogee.

But when you're stuck with being old,
Consolations of a different sort.
You can choose the game to play,
And play it on your homely court.

You can change some of the rules,
And when you take the playing field.
It's much more fun to call the tune,
Your marching band won't have to yield.

Truth be Told

Do you wish to hear the truth?
Are you ready to be shown?
It might not be what you will like,
The consequence is yours alone.

Often we are just pretending,
Things are good for you and me.
Afraid of some dark terror lurking,
Mirrored in reality.

But finally when the truth be told,
When all's stripped bare for all to see.
You cannot hide from what's inside,
Your karma that is meant to be.

Face the facts you cannot flee,
Till God or the Devil sets you free.

Apprehensions from A Nether Place

(Obsessions from the Manic Id)

Not too often – unpredictably only now and then,
I find myself being drawn relentlessly once again,
By some dormant fragment that will
break on through to the other side,
Like some self-addictive past turbulent
afflicted rushing tide.

Sometimes a more innocent and breathless time.
Sometimes some vivid episode without reason or rhyme.
Pregnant with possibility for whatever
calling's meant to be,
And for but a moment the World distilled to my reality.

Such are these sensations - obsessions from the past,
Too intense the feelings – too harmful should they last.
Banish to distant memory - remote
places once well known,
Better off for sanity - leave well enough alone.

After the Fall

How brave the heroic progenitor's soul,
That crawled by choice from tribal bliss.
Lost he stumbled with all amiss,
Till falling upon an emergent goal.

Awareness dawned frail and alone,
Change he must to better survive.
With faltering steps he stayed alive,
And staggered toward dreams that were unknown.

He's responsible against all odds,
For all he's able to achieve.
And moving forward he must believe,
He will approach his self-made Gods.

The Transcendental Man

Whither Transcendental Man,
Able to peer through time and space.
Knows beginning and the end,
Have we looked him in the face?

Did he visit Bethlehem,
Lo those many years ago.
Or is he conjured in our minds,
To ease the lives that come and go?

Or will our calculating brains,
Prove with perfect certainty.
That we are all transcendent men,
Reaching for shared reality.

The Lost Word

What was spoken long ago?
Long before the Written Word.
And its meaning who will know?
Since no one's left who may have heard.

Myths were started by renown,
Lost in antiquated mist.
Often distorted as passed on,
Deliberate with an ambiguous twist.

So beware of prior sophistry,
Meant to entangle you in lies.
Be skeptical of history,
When written by misleading eyes.

Vanishing Point

Are you among the fortunate few –
disappearing into the present?
Abandoning past and future – if but only for a moment.
If so then you are truly Tuesday's Child,
Full of grace – radiant with the joy of being.

Or did you lose that magic long ago?
Replaced with ties to times other than Now.
Restraining you from madness and the most,
Now a bland observer of Life's games swirling about.

Do you seek shelter in the spectator's role?
Fortune's slings and arrows exact no toll.
Blanketed by a numbing serenity,
Insulated from high anxiety.

Or do you want your senses revived?
With quickening pulse you come alive.
Find someone or something to be your new scope,
And vanish within is your last and best hope.

The Siren's Song

Do you have a siren's song?
Some enchanted calling you must obey.
Its message urgent you cannot delay,
Leading you to where you know you belong.

Only a few are possessed by a Muse,
Mostly to life we turn a tin ear.
What life has to tell we often don't hear,
We end up with nothing to gain or to lose.

So listen to life that is swirling about,
Surely there's something that captivates you.
Something surprising assuring and new,
And suddenly something you can't be without.

The Road Less Traveled

When did you first begin to see,
How difficult to exceed mediocrity?
Distance a near infinity,
Rising an inch is a struggle for me.

Certainly not seen in youth's gaiety,
Protected by its self-proclaimed immortality.
Nor seen in adult complexity,
Often distracted by its hubris of certainty.

Better left for the clarity of a latter day's advice,
Transfixed by genius and sacrifice.
The road to greatness cannot be traveled twice,
And the toll you pay exacts a heavy price.

Mediocrity's Stepchild

Numbers always tell the score,
But they can't reach infinity.
They can't even get up close,
By using only 1,2,3...

The same applies to you and me,
Reaching beyond our mundane place.
I've looked inside for what I need,
I haven't found a single trace.

And I have tried a lot of things,
In each I did not get too far.
But what if I add up all my scores?
I'm sorry to say it's barely par.

Brilliance and genius are rarified gifts,
Have it and use it and reach for beyond.
And cast your enchanted spell on the world,
I'm in awe of those gifted wherever they're found.

Great Expectations

Do some memories past bring you wisps of remorse?
You lived through those times expectations so great.
You pushed to the limit impatience wouldn't wait.
How different the outcome as your play runs its course.

But someday you'll see imperfection allowed.
Reaching perfection might not bring you more.
Some battles were lost but you didn't lose the war.
Your courage though tested still strong and unbowed.

So be pleased with the times you put up a good fight.
No matter the outcome you did all you could.
Intentions and efforts were all to the good.
Take retiring bow and exit stage right.

Just Do It

(to the Movers and Shakers)

Do not seek permission, just do what you must do.
Do not expect external praise, no
one knows better than you.
Do not look for certainty, it never will show through.
Do not wait for fate-filled signs, you'll never have a clue.

Alas no magic guides our path, as
promised in distant Youth.
No one is chosen in advance, that's the unspoken truth.
So think enough for reason's sake,
then act and follow through.
There's time enough at a later date, To hold it in review.

These thoughts are meant for everyone,
and that simply is because.
It's better to be a has been, than become a never was.

Past Remembrance

Oh for a child's joy and innocence, when magic in the air!
Or youth's thriving excitement, opportunity everywhere!
Or adult's driving passion, no time for despair!
And loved ones still present, in your mind always there!

Search only rarely hear again what they say,
Past touchstones of living that lighted your way.
Feel the glow of remembrance then put them away,
Best left in the past they're not part of today.

But move past remembrance – extend what they mean,
They offer suggestions – from the shadows unseen.
For making the most – though not always first dream,
Of what lies before you – the slate now wiped clean.

Shelter from the Storm

Each of us since we were born,
Is seeking shelter from the storm.
Some thing or place or calming pause,
That grants a purpose to because.

Hard to find still harder to last,
All to soon it rushes past.
Some odd unknown or misplaced should,
And the love of your life is gone for good.

And though alone the remaining while,
There remains for you an inward smile.
A trace of what can't be compared,
The longed-for joy that once was shared.

Make the Most

I've had my chance I've made the most,
Of all those gifts offered to me.
Though average at best and some goals lost,
No complaints that I can see.

When time winds down and it's your turn,
I hope you measure up to say.
Though challenges come you quickly learn,
To push past doubts that block your way.

Afraid to act is often worse,
Win or lose the thrill's the same
So don't be too much risk averse,
Be off the sideline in the game.

Time to Go

I prefer to leave on my own terms,
And on a chosen day.
When interest in Life gives no returns,
And there's nothing left to say.

When all affairs are neatly done,
Still able to go my own way.
One lasting glance at setting Sun,
I prefer not to lengthen the stay.

When those once loved no longer living,
And remembrance a whisper of pain.
I can pretend with brief thanksgiving,
To see them once again.

Shed nary a tear this once promising fellow,
Has come to the end of his run.
To all he has cared for a wish made when callow,
Please pardon the wrongs he has done.

www.ingramcontent.com/pod-product-compliance
Lightning Source LLC
Chambersburg PA
CBHW030913080526
44589CB00010B/287